PERCEIVING PURPOSE

Sanjay Gupta

INTELLECTUAL PRESS
375 Park Avenue
Suite 2607
New York, New York 10152

Books may be purchased in quantity and/or special sales by
contacting Intellectual Press at ip@intellectualpress.com or by
calling 212-498-9272

[1. Philosophy 2. Psychology]

First Edition

ISBN: 978-1-946670-02-1

10 9 8 7 6 5 4 3 2 1

Special thanks to Nicholas J. Davis and Alexander Honkala

DEDICATION

In memory of Cody and Vito, who showed me purpose;

To my parents, who gave me every opportunity to realize it.

For my children, so they might discover their own.

CONTENTS

INSCRIPTION

"What I really need is to get clear about what I must do, not what I must know, except insofar as knowledge must precede every act. What matters is to find a purpose, to see what it really is that God wills that I shall do; the crucial thing is to find a truth which is truth for me, to find the idea for which I am willing to live and die."

Søren Kierkegaard

Sanjay Gupta

PREFACE

This book wouldn't be complete if I didn't tell you about its silent co-author, my dog Cody. He is the inspiration for so many of the ideas here, so I think it is only fair that I tell you a little bit about him.

Cody was two-years old when I adopted him from the local pound in 2005. He was a gorgeous tricolor Basset who had been surrendered along with a whole litter of puppies that he had fathered, and his female 'companion.' (I was never told about his marital status — even dogs have some privacy rights, apparently). He was the last one remaining of his clan at the pound, and since this was "kill-shelter," he didn't have much longer before his number was up. I needed a dog, and he needed a home. Seemed like a fair trade at the time. I hope he thought so, too.

You like to think that you go to the pound to choose a dog; in Cody's case, I had nothing to do with it. As is often the case at the shelter, the dogs go wild when a visitor comes by, and your heart aches knowing that you can't take them all home — just one, if you are lucky. When he first saw me, he simply walked up to the end of the kennel where I was standing, turned around, and plopped his behind facing me. In dog-language, I have learned that is both a sign of trust — and of ownership. This dog knew that he owned me. What I didn't realize at the time was just how true that really was.

I took Cody everywhere with me. He loved car trips, he liked boats (big boats — he was not fond of canoes), and was fixture at my office. We were pretty much inseparable, and that was just fine by me. He came with me to my new job in California, where he caused all sorts of mischief in the Palo Alto suburb that we had made our home. He was very fond of breaking loose from our fenced yard, and visiting with the neighbors. I remember the time our neighbor found him lying in the middle of our quiet suburban street, just waiting for people to come by and give him a belly-rub. Hardly the smartest place to take a nap — but he always knew how to draw attention to himself, and he trusted everyone to a fault.

Later on, he moved with us to Santa Monica for a new job, and he started to reveal a lot of important truths to me. The job I took was with a brilliant and hard-charging self-made billionaire, and the work was intense. But no matter how crazy my life got, no matter what kind of role I would take for work, he remained a constant reminder of what really mattered most. Cody became a symbol of the things that counted — family, dogs, and a life worth living.

Watching him bask under the rays of the Santa Monica sunshine was immensely therapeutic — it was the definition of peace and tranquility.

We later moved back to Connecticut, and Cody helped fulfill a childhood dream of driving coast-to-coast across the American Heartland with my dog. It is still hard to believe that I fulfilled a dream from my childhood of driving thousands of miles with just my dog and not much else. It was a spiritual journey like no other, and I cherish it still. It is in many ways the catharsis that helped wash away so many illusions about what life was supposed to look like. When you fulfill a dream, you can let go of the petty ambitions that cloud your perception of purpose. You start to realize what is possible, rather than what isn't, and you find a satisfaction within yourself that puts an end to a lot of the self-doubt and false aspirations that we previously believed would make us happy. With Cody riding shotgun, we toured the canyons of Colorado, the desert flats of Nevada, the vast cornfields of Nebraska, and actually saw a pig fly in Indiana —(the pig was being hoisted by a crane from a semi that had flipped over). It was a remarkable journey, and he did his best to navigate, which is to say, snore loudly while he dozed dreamily in the car seat. Frankly, it didn't matter if we got lost — in fact, I sometimes wish that we did, and found a place where dogs never age, and life is all about hanging out with your best friend.

Cody taught me what my purpose in life was and still is — to be a steward, and a servant, in the best tradition that dogs have shown us through their loyalty and patience with everything they do. He taught me the meaning of humility and respect, and what it meant to care for those who could not care for themselves. There is no doubt in my mind that Cody gently instructed me on how to be a better father, and a better person, by quietly revealing his own perception of purpose.

Cody passed away on May 19, 2016 after a long illness which he endured with such stoic pride and selflessness, it forced me to put all of my petty concerns in perspective. It was the hardest day of my life, and I still can't talk about him without choking up, so forgive me for not talking about him more — the emptiness of his dog bed, which is now home to one of our elderly cats, is a harsh reminder of the cruelest part of life — losing someone you love. I can't fathom the pain that others endure in their own lives with the horrible things that go on in this world, but I can tell you that I have a lot more empathy as a result of knowing what it feels like to have a part of you torn out, leaving a hole that you know can't be filled, and shouldn't. Some things just can't be healed — and we shouldn't pretend that we can. You need to know pain in order to experience joy, and that little Basset Hound surely gave me lessons in both.

All I can do now is remember my best friend, and try to honor his memory by sharing with the world everything that he tried to teach me. Dogs have so much wisdom, so much kindness, and so much truth within their souls. They give everything to us, and don't ask for much in return. Just our love, our respect, and the noblest parts of the human spirit — and we should do everything we can to learn from their example in a world that doesn't seem to understand the value of honesty, or what it really stands for.

The world would be a better place if we all understood what was truly important to each of us individually. We can't make good choices unless we look deeply within ourselves to understand what guides our decisions and our actions. I have a feeling that a lot of problems that we face today are borne of self-ignorance, because we wouldn't make the same choices if we actually examined them within the frame of what we know intuitively is right, but fail to act, or look the other way. Whether by an innate sense of what is right or wrong, or a level of introspection that we simply fail to recognize, dogs seem to have the upper hand when it comes to knowing the nature of things, and what is *truly* important. Dogs teach us about life's purpose and how we can understand what that means for each of us individually — we just have to have the courage to look at ourselves, and face our own truth.

-Sanjay Gupta

Perceiving Purpose

CHAPTER ONE

Introduction

INTRODUCTION

This book is about hope. And the mind of a Basset Hound.

When you realize that 'advice' is not the same thing as 'insight', you are ready to read this book. If you have read book after book looking for answers, but still remain confused about why the matters of your life continue to be at odds with one another, it is not because of the seemingly obvious issues of money or time. They are symptoms of a perceptual blindness to one's purpose. Within the context of this book, purpose is an intellectually tangible concept that can be deconstructed, analyzed and realized. It is not an abstract notion to be cast about like a meaningless object. It is a thing that you can dissect, understand, and control, and be used to guide your life. All that is required of you is a few hours of quiet reflection, and pencil and paper.

My problem is likely very similar to your own — no matter where we come from, how we were raised, or what we do, we all face the same existential quandaries. I believe that when we shed the blinders that obscure us to our own conception of self, we can get closer to what matters most. What makes us different is probably the volume of work and study I wasted in pursuing answers to these questions; I began my study of these questions at the age of 13, and haven't stopped for 30 years. What bothers me is that despite all our advances as a society, instead of getting "smarter", we appear to be asking the wrong questions, and tend to pursue inflated ideas. I'm all for simple. I use dogs as my model for introspective inquiry, since it is clear that writing a bigger treatise with ever bigger words is not going solve our existential dilemmas. Besides, I've always wanted to create a school of thought. Dognosticism!

The desire to find purpose in one's life might seem daunting at first. The weight of your many responsibilities and relationships may cloud your thinking, and it might not be immediately clear what steps you need to take in order to pursue meaningful change. Others even dissuade you from even making the attempt, claiming it is a selfish exercise. Ignorance of oneself is one of the surest paths to misery and continued self-loathing. Self examination is not a sin — it a right, and a virtue. I will show you how.

Unlike most books on the topic transformation, this one will not drag on for hundreds of pages. In fact, you'll spend less than an hour to read the two main concepts and can start using them immediately. My message to you is that this is not complicated, completely attainable, and that real change can take place immediately.

Everything in this book is rooted in the truth that one finds from years of agonizing self-doubt, self-inquiry, and staring into the soulful eyes of a canine companion who seems to have all the answers. Though simple on its face, this book is informed by the philosophy of Aristotle, Kierkegaard, Kant, and Nietzsche, all of whom wrestled with the purpose and meaning of life and are widely admired for their contributions. Using their wisdom as a guide, and the mind of a dog as a model, the process of introspective inquiry is applied to transform your life in practical terms, to elicit that which is most meaningful in your life, and what is aligned to your own perception of purpose.

I've done this countless times with people. It is fascinating, and incredibly illuminating, for both me and the individual, to see how their conception of self, expressed in the form of their sense of purpose, is often at complete odds with the basic structure of their lives, the people they associate with, or the things they do. The hardest part about doing this exercise is turning away from it; once you see what is lying just outside your conscious self, it is hard to not keep looking, and re-evaluating. It becomes a continuous sub-conscious and mechanical process, and I believe it is the same process that informs the consciousness of dogs that makes them so uniquely honest and humble — and reliable — as companions and friends. Once we see that within ourselves, we latch onto to it — with everything we have.

I call this type of consciousness *'perceiving dog.'* I hope you benefit from their wisdom as much as I have.

Thanks for joining me.

ORIGIN OF PURPOSE

I FIRST realized that my dog knew more about life than I did after I observed him snoozing in his bed by the fire during the holidays. No matter what kind of chaos might erupt around the house, no matter what demands a child or a spouse might have, no matter what was going on with work, the world, or the furnace, there was a contentment to just "being there", warm, and near his family, that was undeniable. If that dog could know peace amidst all this chaos, why couldn't the rest of us? Chaos, I learned, is as much a physical reality that we can do nothing about, as well as an emotional response. The dog chooses to not respond. Amazing.

Clearly, that dog knew also knew more about *how* to live life at this point than I did as well. I thought about it at length, but when you reduce whatever is going on in the dog's mind compared to what we believe we perceive as reality, the thing that makes us the same is "purpose". Whatever my dog's conception of purpose, he seemed more than content with it; moreover, the elements of his life were aligned it as well. It was dreadfully simple; you could argue that the dog knows less about the world, or has less ability to reason, but that is intellectually arrogant and subjective. Instead of asserting some kind of intellectual superiority over presumedly lesser-thinking creatures, true humility demands that you inspect what can be learned. What does the dog know that you don't? What makes you the same as the dog? Turning to some Aristotelian philosophy, I ended back up where I started at the beginning of my education — the idea of purpose, or what is your end — or in Greek, your *telos.*

If we were to summarize what makes up our purpose, there could be an argument that stretches across the ages, but reflecting upon the life of my dog, I chose to see what could be reduced that was the same. We both had **Values** — (he was a "good boy", or at least, aspired to be - and I wanted to be a "good person"); we both had **Goals** (gnawing through that giant rawhide, or the couch, or a shoe, or...and I certainly had aspirations, like overcoming my fear of sushi); we both had **Beliefs** (as a conscious creature, a dog certainly has beliefs — what those are, we can't quite know for sure, but when you stare into their eyes for a few hours, you become convinced of their inner wisdom; I certainly have beliefs); and lastly, we both had **Roles.** For him, he had the role of being the chief plate-licker and house-greeter and bed-warmer; as for me; well, the list is long, and gets longer every day, it seems, but it always seems to be end with the phrase "Amount Due Now".

While the model for the elements of purpose could be argued axiomatically on these grounds alone, we can also see dramatic similarities between its core aspects and the main traditions of philosophical inquiry:

- **Values** - Virtue, Morality, Ethics
- (Aristotle, Kant, Hegel, Socrates, Nietzsche...)

- **Beliefs** - Epistemology, Perception, "Knowing"
- (Hume, Descartes, Spinoza)

- **Goals** - Logic, Reasoning, Rationalization
- (Boole, Aristotle)

- **Role** - Identity, often reasoned through Metaphysics
- (Heidegger, Leibniz, Aristotle)

In this sense, you have your choice — you can go with a purely reductionist view of purpose through the lens of brute honesty, (the dog), or you can model purpose on the back of thousands of years of philosophical inquiry, all of which has more or less ended up in the same four quadrants of self-concept. I choose the dog. Life is too short to live it locked away in the Ivory tower.

Moving along, I also looked carefully at what my dog did differently with regard to sensing his purpose compared with my own. My conclusion was simply this. Dogs don't **lie**. People, on the other hand, are experts at deceiving not only others, but themselves in particular. The essential difference between the happy dog and the miserable human is that the dog doesn't need to lie about what is important to him; he is willing to admit what he likes and doesn't like. Humans, on the other hand, are constantly making excuses to cover up the reality of their conscious behavior, and is perpetually at war with its subconscious self. It was time to start thinking more like the dog, I reasoned.

The dog has so many advantages over the human from a lifestyle perspective — but all kidding aside, in a very serious way, their chief advantage is the discipline of self-interest or, put another way, a complete disinterest in lying to themselves about what is important to them. That does not mean that dogs, as a rule, never act against their self-interest; on the contrary, examples of bravery, loyalty, and manifest duty are all evidence of how the dog perceives its purpose. As I started to understand this, it became clear that the framework for breaking down the truth of our own purpose was necessary because we are highly disadvantaged as a species compared with our canine companions. While truth comes naturally to them, this is something we have to re-learn as comparatively inferior 'sentient' humans.

'*Perceiving dog*', as I like to jokingly call it, does not come naturally to us. As such, we need a framework for breaking down and digesting our perceived sense of purpose in order to realize transformation.

These elements need to interrogated by your own conscience systematically and understood in order for you to get to the heart of what makes your mind and your soul tick. Purpose is often used generically in most management and self-help theory; take your pick of best practices, and most of them will have the word "purpose" worked into their rhetoric. Within the genre of religious self-help, it is not much more helpful, but offered up as a divine mystery that should not be questioned. My issue with contemporary management thinking, agnostic 'mindfulness', and religious dogma today is that most of it has gotten away from the basic elements of how to conduct a self-examination of one's beliefs; we have lost the art of self-reflection. We ignore this reflective exercise at our peril, because this is the same information we need in order to make decisions on a daily basis about what is important, and what is not. Not knowing what is important versus what is within the context of your purpose leads to massive waste in time and energy, which is one of the reasons you are probably seeking transformation in your life, as I have.

What I offer in this book is a mirror into your own self, using the tools of critical self-examination that you already have, but have been taught to let go by years of evasion and circumstance that cloud the your reason. It is for this reason that this book is about how to dissect your own beliefs, rather than foist mine upon yours.

WHAT TO EXPECT

This book is intended to be a fast read, and to get you down to business in short order. My dogs didn't have a lot of patience during dinner time (or at any other time, for that matter) — and I learned a noble truth in that — we waste time deliberating when we could be acting. Dogs like to act, even when they are sleeping. Sleeping, I learned, *is* an act.

To make things simple, think of this book as a user manual. There are two parts to this system, the **Inquiry**, which is you asking questions of yourself, and the **Inventory**, which is you taking note of your world and yourself as you perceive them. The book explains the various pieces that make up both ideas in each part of the system. In the **Inquiry**, we have the elements of Purpose, which are your **Values, Goals, Beliefs,** and **Role,** and within the **Inventory,** you have simple questions from logical theory — does something relate to one (or more) or your elements of purpose, or not.

Following the discussion of both the Inquiry and Inventory, I offer advice on how to complete both, using my own answers to the questions as an example. With the example fresh in your mind, you are asked a few basic questions, which require only paper and pencil. There is no exam, no quiz, and absolutely no homework!

Using your own answers to the Inquiry, you can then start doing your own Inventory, and use a very basic set of your own reasoning and logic, to decide what can stay, and what can go. Dogs seem to be able to do this innately, without much effort. Their ability to discern what is right for them is largely flawless, with notable exceptions, like the time my beagle devoured five-pounds of Chex Mix™ (long story, but hounds like to eat). After you learn the basics, you will do this naturally as well.

THE FOUR ELEMENTS OF PURPOSE

VALUES	GOALS
BELIEFS	ROLE

LOGIC SYMBOLS FOR INVENTORY

$\therefore$	Therefore
$\varnothing$	Irrelevant
$\oplus$	Optional
$\lozenge$	Possible
Δ	Change
$\square$	Necessary
$\cap$	Intersects
$\cup$	Unifies

CHAPTER TWO

Inquiry

THE INQUIRY

The **Inquiry** is a systematic breakdown of your purpose into its four constituent elements: values, beliefs, goals, and role.

The purpose of the inquiry is to force oneself to elicit their assumed understanding of each one of the core areas, as well as identify the correlating opposing ideas in contrast. For example, You are asked not only what values you have, but also, what you stand against; in this way, the individual is able to question whether or not they actually have that value, or in fact, are simply opposed to it intellectually.

This has the effect of opening the mind and ridding assumptions, which is the goal. As assumptions are brought forth, challenged, and then struck down one by one, the individual gets closer and closer to their conception of self, their own ideas of what they actually believe, versus what they thought they believed. This forms a critical base for the next step, the Inventory, which further builds upon your work in the Inquiry. The Inventory will function in proportion to how honest you are in the Inquiry, so you stand much more to gain by being honest with yourself, than not.

The next few pages will give you a few prompts about how to interrogate yourself on these basic ideas of self.

VALUES

WHAT do you stand for? What do you stand against? What are your core values? Why is this important?

Your value system is your own; it could be something your learned from your parents, from religious training, or from your own self-examination. Aristotle's four cardinal virtues – Prudence, Temperance, Justice, and Courage, are but four examples of core values that one can examine within the philosophical canon; there are myriad others to consider within the context of your life and what seems relevant to you.

What values you choose are an important statement about what you believe is most essential as a matter of morality for yourself, as much as it might be for others. If "Prudence" were a crucial value to you, it might indicate that thoughtful deliberation rather than rash action, was something that you sought in yourself, as well as in others. In not finding it in others, you might not identify as well with another individual who might not share the same core values as yourself.

You might find that certain values that you identify with are not necessarily the same things you strongly stand against; in that sense, you might find kinship with individuals who do think differently than you, but share enough of your moral framework to make a relationship purposeful and relevant. This is certainly evident among dogs with different sensibilities; some are fair-minded at play time and will share a chew toy, others are aggressive and cannot bear the thought of doing so.

Too often, we trap ourselves in relationships and associations that do not honor our values, but we don't know why; understanding what you stand for, and stand against, will help you see those differences more clearly, and why certain things work, and other things do not.

What is important to note within identifying your values is that this not a contest for yourself in moral vanity; there are no prizes for enumerating every virtue you "think" is good good, or to identify all things in the world that see as bad; rather, this is about what actually identifies with you personally. On its face, there are probably going to be a great number of things that you will identify as reflexively "good" within your personal value system, whether this is "charity" or "self-sacrifice" or "honesty" , "integrity". Indeed, all are good — but what you stand against should be revealing to you in how strong, or weak, your particular views are, on a given set of values. This is not about what is good or bad in the world; this is about what *you* stand for and against. This is an important distinction.

GOALS

IDENTIFYING your goals and your fears helps put your purpose in perspective. A goal is something you tell yourself you are seeking or reaching for; a fear is something you are avoiding, or a fate you dread. You can't truly understand one, without knowing the other.

You might state that your goal is to spend more time with a specific family member, but the choices you make in and around your life are anything but compatible with that ideal. Reconciling this isn't merely a matter of priorities or fitting "more in" or "doing more with less" – it is cutting away those things that have *nothing* to do with what you want, and doing more about the things you *do* want. Learning how to say "no", and knowing the reason why, will guide your time more purposefully.

Evaluating the underlying intent of your goals is also revealing about aspects of yourself that might have been hidden from view, but need to be addressed. If your goals include the accretion of wealth and power, that is fine – but why? What are your motives? Or if your goal is cure all disease, you must again ask yourself – is this a noble aim, or are your motives borne of ego centrism and megalomania? If that is the case, are those values aligned with your purpose?

That is not to say that all goals must be shredded out of cynicism and self-doubt, but the thoughtful person will interrogate herself, and ask – where did this goal come from, and why? Is this what I truly want? If it isn't, what does inspire me?

Finally, understanding what you *fear* will help sharpen the truth of your goals. You might find that your goal might not be to wealthy after all, but you fear poverty. The accretion of wealth in that context, is not a goal; freedom, however, might be.

My Basset Hound provided amazing insights into this notion of goal versus fear. When we first adopted him, we learned that he had the most profound fear of the garage; he could not bear to go near it. He would dig in his paws and do everything he could to avoid it, even if it meant only getting into the car, which was one of his favorite things to do. Inasmuch as my Basset loved road trips and hanging his droopy ears out the window of the car, the necessity of going through the garage was against the fiber of his being; it was something that stood in the way of one of his cherished goals, despite the seeming irrationality of it.

To me, as a human, it seemed perfectly obvious that

the end result would still be the same — he would get into the car, and he would ultimately be happy. But to him, the fear of going through the garage, irrational though it seemed, was inconsistent with his goals, even if it still resulted in getting into the car.

My dog's behavior revealed two subtle truths for me; we need to be aware of our fears in order to actually pursue our goals fully; but on a moral level, in spite of the reward, there was nothing that could change this dog's mind about what his will would be about that garage — it was a matter of principle. Who knows what my dog actually thought about principle versus fear; only he can tell us, which is why we have to observe their logic and action with humility rather than with arrogance in order to learn.

What is clear, however is that we are very often asked to do things in pursuit of a "goal" that is in contravention of a principle that we know is wrong; and yet, we do it anyway. Wars have been fought and many lives have been lost because of this rationalization. We also shy away from the pursuit of our goals because of the things that we fear. The difference here is in acknowledging our reality, versus blindly accepting it as it is. Fortunately for my dog, I was willing to pull the car out until he got older and wiser, and realized that nothing bad was going to happen with his new family in the garage anymore. But for us humans — we have to do this for ourselves, the deprogramming process, bit by bit, or for each other, if we recognize it in someone we care about.

BELIEFS

WHAT do you believe in, and why? Do you believe in God? Do you believe in Civil Society? Are you a Capitalist? A Democratic-Socialist?

Why is this important? Understanding the origin, conception and reason for our beliefs is a critical aspect of self-examination, because it goes to the heart of how we come to "know" pretty much everything else in our lives . We need to challenge our belief system, and by no means discard it, but at least interrogate it on the level of where it came from, and how it was formed. Was it installed there yourself, or was it instilled in you by a demanding family? How much of your belief system has been subject to rigorous self-examination and inquiry, the kind of testing that would give you confidence to stand up and defend your beliefs should you need to?

In like fashion, admitting your ignorance is not shameful, it is the height of reason, and the depth of humility. Admitting that there are things that you do not know is a moment of intellectual bravery, and opens you up to new possibilities of learning things that were closed off to you before. You cannot learn about something unless you are first aware of its existence; search your beliefs, and catalog your doubts – together they will offer insight into what guides your thinking, how you make decisions, and what you might have missed previously.

When you have dissected the origin of your beliefs, and admitted the breadth of your ignorance, you will understand how certain opportunities in life now have specific relevance to your purpose. You will see more clearly the connection between people, events, and experiences that either bolster or challenge your beliefs, or fill in the gaps of your ignorance – but most importantly, you will see how the world fits in with your reality, and how you can move more assertively, rather than groping in the dark, like an aimless wanderer. Everything you do will now be connected to a purpose.

I found evidence of this in how my dogs used their objectivity to guide their choices. What I found wonderfully erudite about my dogs in their objectivity in sensing the world was their willingness to not merely assume that the "thing" that looked the "same thing before" was indeed "the same thing before". And by this, I mean, anything. It could be a tennis ball, a dog cookie, a chew toy, a raw hide — anything. By and large, my dogs would very carefully analyze the item, carefully considering it (usually by nose) a few sniffs here and there, to confirm "yes" this "thing" is indeed the "same thing" as the thing they encountered before.

This goes to the heart of our belief structure, and how we evaluate information and our world. We process information based upon our beliefs, and what we take to be inherently true, or false. Reconciling what is true or false without first examining its underlying truth, at least on occasion, is dangerous for a great many reasons. We find ourselves in all sorts of trouble as a result of it — we find problems in our institutions, in our government, in our charities, in our schools, among things we believe in, among people we trust — all because we fail to rigorously evaluate what it is we believe, and why. We should always be prepared to defend the things we believe in vigorously — that should never be a question. Just like the dog, who has no doubt the tennis ball is ripe for chewing, it should be a problem for us to defend a thing or an institution that is important to us. But how many things or people can we actually say that we know at the level of certainty now, and are prepared to put our name to?

The contemporary relevance of this problem is all too obvious. We live in an age of 'Fake News" and "Alternative Facts" — and it is impossible for us to evaluate the truth of what we see, if we do not know what is true about ourselves.

In the age of Facebook and Twitter, Instagram and Snapchat, where "friends" come virtually and in the thousands, how many do you actually know, or could defend, if you needed to? How many could defend you? My dog wouldn't chew a tennis ball without first confirming its "nature"; how much diligence do most people conduct in confirming Facebook 'friend' or LinkedIn "contacts"?

When you think critically about yourself, you will start to guard yourself against lies and misrepresentations. You will be able to dissect the intent and underlying agenda of people around you, of the news you read, the ideas that are "sold" to you.

The 'tyranny of ignorance' is most insidious cancer of the human condition. We can only prevail, if we first look within ourselves.

ROLE

WHOM do you serve? WHOM *should* you serve?

In the "Birth of Tragedy", Nietzsche cites an immensely humorous but macabre passage from Greek antiquity, which loosely symbolizes mankind's quest meaning. King Midas sets out on a quest to hunt the wise Silenus to learn what is "best for man". Having captured him, he poses he question, but is unexpectedly met with derision and scorn and is told that short of not being born, the next best thing for man is "to die soon". I somehow doubt this is the wisdom that was being sought, nor was it terribly satisfying to Nietzsche. On the contrary.

It is often said that neither Theologians nor Philosophers like Nietzsche have satisfied the question "purpose", with some defaulting to axiomatic claims that it is simply a matter of divine will, and that it is not a matter of personal concern. Though he is often associated with nihilistic thought, Nietzsche's goes to great lengths to illuminate *purpose* as an existential ideal, as a reason for being. Embedded within this notion of purpose is the idea of role, or service. Serving oneself for Nietzsche is not in and of itself a morally bankrupt ideal; but not knowing who you serve and why, is the object of our concern. Kierkegaard conceptualized his role as service to God, but was insistent that he understand what God's will was nonetheless; it was for him to learn, and could not be assumed. It demanded introspection.

The role you occupy in life will shift from time to time. You might be a student in one scenario, and an executive in another. You might be a patient in one setting, and a caregiver in another. Your *telos*, or end, is the Aristotelian ideal that conceptualizes the greater sum of yourself, but it is hard to qualify in practical terms as your role might change from time to time. It is not necessary for you to know what your role as a human over the length of your life, but rather to understand why you occupy the role you are in now, or should perhaps occupy a different role entirely. Suggesting that your existence is given meaning by divine will might be true, but even theologians recognize that such a dogmatic view is impractical on its face. You have a duty to ask questions, and understand what your role is, and why.

When you identify what it is you do, and whom it is that you serve, you will be able to connect those things that are relevant to that purpose versus everything that is not. In like fashion, understanding who or what you *should* serve might give you greater insight into where to direct your energy, your time, and your attention, as you evaluate the myriad opportunities and demands that are foisted upon you every day. Some will intersect, some will conjoin directly, others will be completely irrelevant – but at least you can decide what is truly relevant and purposeful, and what is not.

In observing my dogs, I saw how their roles were not reductive, but actually, instructive. Instead of looking at the relative simplicity of their actions, which seems to be a prevailing view, we need to be more open to the lessons that we can learn from their example. The maternal instinct that we hear about so often, and laud as an example of the unique role that mothers play from species to species, is always reduced to this base idea that it is an animalistic response — as though the innate nature of protecting one's young is something that we take for granted. But when we extend out that idea of 'protection' as a role — at what point are you willing to sacrifice your notion of what is worth 'protecting' at the expense of some other thing? We rationalize our actions far too often, when in fact, that rationalization is not really grounded in any kind of truth, but a kind of moral convenience that is very often at odds with your perception of purpose. We see so many examples of dogs in nature, risking their lives to save not only their human companions, but also other dogs as well, or even other animals. What guides their sense of purpose? Reduce it as much as you like, but I choose to look at their behavior instructively. However 'simple' the mind of a dog, one thing seems clear — they don't have any conflict in own idea of role. They act against their own self-interests. They defend the things they care about. They know who they are. Do we?

The important thing is to keep in mind who you serve and why; while it might seem incredibly important at the time to shush your child during a work-related call during dinner, the reality is somewhat more perverse. As you reflect on what is most important to you personally, and given the sample of what I have learned from most of the people I have interviewed over the years, most people count spending "more time with their family" versus "working more" as the bigger goal, the bigger priority, hands down. Yet, when you match up action against "role", it never adds up. One of the reasons why is, we lose sight of the very thing we are trying to serve in the first place — the family, or the child. It seems terribly ironic, but we often end up neglecting the child or spouse in the name of "work" — and then wonder why the child acts up, or the spouse does something worse. This is largely because we fail to ask this other question — whom *should* I serve, after we look at answering the question of who we are serving.

Role is complex because it often involves so many others, and managing the dynamics of those relationships is of course complicated. A fascinating insight into how you intersect with someone close to you, however, is actually comparing the results of your Inquiry and Inventory with that of your partner. (I had always hoped to experiment with dogs, but the closest I could get was doggy day camp).

Of all the questions in the Inquiry, I get pressured on role the most, because of the practical reality that is concomitant with balancing "work" and everything else. My response is simply this — there is no "silver bullet" to erase the practical reality of work from our lives, but we can certainly eliminate everything else that is irrelevant and meaningless from our sense of purpose that has nothing to do with the things we actually care about. We can learn a great deal from the example set by our dogs — and I learned quickly that my Basset Hound would not do anything he didn't want, but would imperil himself to safeguard the the people and things that were important to him. He knew, whether introspectively or intuitively, what as important to him, and what his unique role was. I still have a lot to learn about my own, but I continue to try.

That is the point of transforming our lives through introspection; it is only honest reflection and self-inquiry that we can derive what is actually important, and what is not, and start to say "no" to the things that add nothing to our lives (or take away), and start eliminating those things that drain the limited time and resources that we do have from the things we do cherish. In a less trivial sense, it extends beyond the thoughtless waste of time and money, but also what ideals we feel a duty to guard, and what transgressions we must fight against. Knowing your role is one thing — but actually acting upon it will require courage. And many of us are facing tests of that courage in our present reality.

CHAPTER THREE

Inventory

THE INVENTORY

The **Inventory** is the practical application of your perception of purpose within your daily life. Simply stated, it is a model of thought that can be used to assess the relevance of different things in your life — your relationships, the activities you spend time on, and the things you own.

The goal of the Inventory is to look critically at all choices we make about the things within our lives, and see whether these choices are actually aligned with our perception of purpose. It relies heavily on the level of honesty you are willing to commit to yourself in conceiving the four elements of your purpose. Without that basic honesty, we cannot truly assess the relevance of what it is we do, whom we interact with, or what we own (or want to own), if it is not guided by self-knowledge.

This goes to the very heart of self-examination and transformation as a potential in our lives. With the Inventory, we can gauge what is true for us, and know why, rather than blindly edging along the path. Very often, that blindness leads us to make decisions that are not only misaligned with our perception of purpose, but directly antithetical to it as well.

The Inventory is best understood by evaluating the things that ordinarily confuse our perception of purpose without critical self-examination. These elements include Ignorance, or expressed another way, our perception of reality; our Intent, or what truly motivates our decisions; our Will, or whether we choose to have freedom of choice, or give it away; and lastly, Honesty, or the fidelity that we have to ourselves and to one another.

The following is a reflection on the challenges that each of these elements present in the course of self-examination, and what we need to be aware of in order to overcome them.

IGNORANCE / PERCEPTION

A fundamental truth of the human condition is its unwillingness to confront reality; the mind would rather lie to itself and others to preserve an illusion than confront harsh truths. We do this reflexively as a learned trait, and unlearning it is a process that takes discipline and commitment. Being honest about what you truly want or truly believe is the first step in realizing the truth of what causes you pain, or what truly gives you joy. In the same sense, it is *because* of dishonesty that we are blind to that which makes us miserable. Alcoholics don't get better just because they quit drinking; they recover when they stop lying – and simple honesty is what separates a recovering alcoholic from the self-righteous dry-drunk who can admit no wrong, and insists they cause no harm.

The process of knowing yourself is never an easy exercise, and introspection is hard-fought and as individual as anything you can imagine. Yet, reflecting on **why** you do a certain thing, and then assessing whether it aligns with your values, beliefs, and your role, is, is an important step in eliminating waste from your day, and from your life.

For dogs, this obviously comes naturally. In observing them, you come to realize that they have a basic honesty about their behavior that allows them to be free about their likes and dislikes, what they will eat, and what they will bite (or perhaps, just growl at). In all seriousness, however, that seemingly simplistic aspect to their nature is something we need to take note of in our own lives; a basic honesty in what we say, do, think and feel.

Understanding how our time is governed is rooted in how we perceive who controls it, and why. It seems evident that dogs don't anything that they don't want to; this is particularly true of Basset Hounds. I offer you a simple way to dissect how you perceive how your time is governed. In this book, you will find two blank charts, one that represents your typical day as you currently know it, and another as you would ideally like it. Mark it up the first with your activities (work, play, school, obligations, yoga, beer pong, whatever) and then make a note — what part of your purpose is it aligned with? Is this on your calendar by your choice, or because someone put it there?

On the ideal scenario, do the same thing — and again, mark up the activities with elements of your purpose. Are they aligned?

Don't be surprised if your "real" calendar contains a number of things that don't line up with your purpose as you understand it; but if your "ideal" calendar doesn't match up with your purpose at all, you might have to check some of your assumptions. What was it about those activities that appealed to you? What was it about the elements of purpose that you missed, or that you might not have been completely honest about?

On a more practical level, the next time someone asks for your time – ask yourself first, with everything else that is demanded of me, with everything that I demand of myself, with everything that I wish to give to others, can I afford to give this time?

Offering your time without first considering its cost or implications to yourself and others is both foolish and dishonest. There is nothing noble about being generous with something you have so little of; you will either be in debt to yourself or to another, it will come at some cost to someone.

The basic idea is — if a given thing, person, event, role, etc. is not aligned in some fashion with one of the four elements of your purpose — namely your values, goals, beliefs or role, then it is likely a waste of your time at best, or possibly damaging at worst.

The transformational aspect of introspection is the

realization that the decisions that we make on a daily basis are made largely out of ignorance of our own self-interest; in not knowing ourselves, we make bad decisions, which compound upon themselves, and increase our misery and pain.

If you have the self-awareness of knowing what is aligned with your purpose, and can defend your time accordingly, you stand a better chance of not squandering your days; if you know what your values and beliefs are, as well as what they are not, you will have an easier time of saying "no" instead of reflexively saying "yes" to every question that demands your time or your resources.

At the end of this text, there are example pages that offer samples of what you can use to create your own inventories of ideas or things to measure against your Inquiry, and determine what can stay, and what can go.

INTENT / MOTIVATION

WHAT motivates you and why? Why do you do the things you do? Why do you associate with the people that you do? Why do you want certain things?

Dissecting intent is one of the of the most difficult exercises an individual can undertake. Exposing the true reason why you do a certain thing, and examining its motive, is often impossible for most, and for those achieve any degree of success, there is a stark realization – it is a process, you will never be perfect, and you will always be on guard against the theft of your time once you learn how it is stolen.

I offer rudimentary logic and set theory to merge the elements of purpose in a practical way. It is simple and easy to understand. The set you define are the elements of your purpose — your Values, Roles, Beliefs, and Goals (V, R, B, G). Either something is ⊘ "Irrelevant" or it is ☐ "Necessary". You can decide how fine you want to thread the needle - I offer the basics of symbolic logic here in this book for you to consider if you like. I prefer binary "yes/no" decisions in my assessments. Others I have talked with are capable of incredibly complex computations — it is really based on your preference. But with this basic system, you will be shocked how quickly you can assess whether any given thing, person or activity can be assessed within the four elements of your purpose, and why something that didn't seem to make sense to you before, now suddenly might.

Once complete, you will have taken the first step of many that you will do each day in evaluating the relevance of the things, people, and events that clamor for your time. Only you can decide what is relevant to your purpose, what is meaningful, and what is worthy; but the inventory will serve as your initial guide to understanding what you have committed to and why, and whether it is truly connected to your ultimate purpose.

If you find things that are not, don't be alarmed – consider yourself lucky. You will have proved a valuable thing in and of itself — that you are willing to acknowledge a fundamentally difficult tension in your life. Most people cannot face this basic truth; it is too painful. The next step is choosing what you spend your time on, knowing what you have learned about yourself.

Sanjay Gupta

WILL / FREEDOM

OVER the course of time, you will be introduced to many new ideas, and invited to meet many new people. The only thing that stands between you and the squander of your days is your own will.

Dogs seem to have it easy, but when you think about it, there must be a fair amount of anxiety in their daily lives — not knowing when their owner will get back home to walk them, not knowing when they might get food or water, not knowing what will happen when they get in the car (oh no, not the Vet!) — in generally, just not knowing. They have to submit to the reality of leaving so much of their lives to wisdom and care of their owners and caregivers, hoping that they will do the right thing, at the right time. On some level, we have to acknowledge that the dog understands more about the nature of reality than we do. There is only so much we can plan for, and for the rest of it, well — we had better use that time the way we want.

I don't think my dogs really did anything they didn't want, including sleeping — unless it was against their will. The question is, what choices will you make with yours, given that you have so many more choices than a dog? And why would you squander those choices when it is such a precious gift to be able to choose?

Your time is your own, and is your most precious asset. Your attention is the greatest gift you can give to a fellow human being. Ironically, we often neglect our own basic needs, and forget that our minds remain the one constant companion, which you both nourish and placate, lest you lose sight of who you are, and what you intend to be.

As such, you must discern that which you "must" do, and what you "cannot" do; and this becomes an easy exercise when you realize that your time is guided by your purpose, and not merely the hours left in the day.

Take a note when a book is recommended, or when you are recommended to meet someone. Write down the places and things you are encouraged to visit or try, but do not commit until you have a moment to think about how these things fit into your life and your values. And then, add them to your plan when the time is right. It seems silly to think about this now, but how often do we say "sure" when one of our friends or colleagues tells us "oh, you should meet so and so"? The first thing that would come to my mind when someone suggested a play date for my Basset Hound was if the dog would bite my pooch. You can argue this any which way you like, but the reality is that we give little thought to the exponential impact that social introductions have on our lives when have no meaningful intersection of purpose with our own. They take time away from our families, our work, and from our ourselves, if they are not properly aligned.

Very simply, we can actively plan our lives around our purpose, rather than letting others dictate it for us. My dogs lived every moment in the moment, even if they were "just" sleeping. They did what they could to live their lives on their own terms. We could do the same.

HONESTY / FIDELITY

THOUGH much has been written about "success" and how to achieve it, relatively little has been written about failure and how to avoid it. Most individuals will plan their day, and their lives, hoping for success, but will end up miserable because they never examined their underlying motives for doing certain things or reasons for being with certain people.

Examining the root and cause of why and what you do will offer a fundamentally different perspective on the value and usage of time. A moments introspection will reveal where a given thing, individual, or event will fall on your spectrum of relevance. Deciding against that which goes against what you believe, what you value, what your goals are, or what your role is, might be difficult at first, but it is fundamentally *your* choice once you take the step of trying to understand who you are. All it takes is a bit of honesty, and a great deal of courage.

We owe ourselves the dignity of guarding our minds against the incessant demands and controls of an external reality that cares little for individual thought or expression. There is only one person in the world who can truly perform that function with absolute fidelity and precision, and that person can only discharge his or her duty if there is complete honesty in their self-assessment of themselves and what they hold most dear.

If you have a dog (or had a dog) you, you probably know the closest thing to fidelity that a human can conceive, both in spirit and and form. Very likely, if you have similar sensibilities to my own, you would have gladly traded your life for your dog's, should it have become necessary. Most dogs, as you know, would do the same for their owners. That is one of things that guide their purpose; they seem to be defined by need to serve, even if it costs them everything.

To guide your life with purpose, you need only honesty. Think of each day as a page of your life. You are its author. How it connects to every other page, is up to you. Dogs seem to be born with the this innate wisdom of living life purposefully and with honesty to one's self and one's ideals. By discovering your purpose through humility and introspection, you also will be *perceiving dog*.

CHAPTER FOUR

Instructions

A GUIDE ON HOW TO DO THE INQUIRY AND INVENTORY

THE following pages form the core of your introspective inquiry. Using the initial text as a guide, answer the questions the way you see fit.

Some like to do the exercise alone, some like to talk to a friend or someone they deeply trust, but after a time, you will probably find yourself wondering if the answers you wrote down are correct. There are no correct answers, only truthful ones.

When you are satisfied that the answers do represent your values, goals, beliefs and role, then summarize your answers in the ASSESSMENT, which is merely a summary of what you believe makes up the four elements of your purpose. This can change. It may evolve. It probably will. There is no way to get it right, or get it wrong. Change is pretty much the only constant.

After you complete the Inquiry & Assessment, you are ready to do the Inventory. The inventory relies upon Symbolic Logic, beautiful and simple. The diagram key will show you what each symbol means. It is incredibly intuitive – and, of course, logical.

* * *

Using the Inventory, you will be able to discern opportunities from distractions, true relationships from transactional ones, meaningful pursuits from intellectual fictions, and so on. Kant's *Critique of Pure Reason* is the key pillar for the Inquiry; before it, you assumed things to be true; afterwards, you have some idea of what is, and is not, an assumption. It is a start. It is a process. And over time, it will pay off to be honest with yourself about what you know, as well as what you don't.

HOW TO DO THE INQUIRY

THE Inquiry that follows is based upon a few simple questions that are meant to prompt a bit of self-reflection. For some, this will come quite naturally; for others, it might be quite alien.

Instructions:

Materials needed:

- A few blank sheets of paper, or your favorite journal (or use the **Note** pages in this book)
- Your favorite writing instrument, or anything that makes a mark on paper (crayon will do)

Draw the four-quadrants of the Axis of Purpose on a sheet of paper: Values, Goals, Beliefs, and Role. The Inquiry is guided by a set of four simple opposing questions concerning the elements of your purpose (diagram is on page **83**) :

Values:

- What do you stand for?
- What do you stand against?
- Summary: Your core values.

Goals:

- What inspires me?
- What do I fear?
- Summary: My aspirations.

Beliefs:

- What do I believe in?
- What do I doubt?
- Summary: What I must learn.

Role:

- Whom do I serve?
- Whom should I serve?
- Summary: What I must do.

To illustrate how easy this is, I'll offer a bit of proof of the fact that I eat my own "dog food", as it were....here are my answers. There isn't a trick here — it is merely understanding that any conception of an idea that you have is incomplete unless you think of its equal and opposing nature. Would you eat something that tastes good if you knew that it was also poison? A dog would not, but tragically, often does, when it finds spilled antifreeze in a garage, or other chemicals that are appealing to their palate. They will drink it out of ignorance. If their senses gave them the ability to perceive the threat of the poison, they would avoid it, but they lack that capability. Ignorance of oneself is a <u>choice</u>.

My Answers to the Oppositional Questions:

What I stand for:	Honesty Work Peace Solitude Independence Service
What inspires me:	Freedom Education for my children
What do I believe in:	God Dog Freedom of Thought
Whom do I serve?	Employer Government Lawyers Society Authority Banks

* * *

What I stand against:	Arrogance
	Illegitimacy
	Abuse
	False prophets
	Vanity
	Waste
What I Fear:	Control
	Regulation
	Power
	Authority
What I Doubt:	My own senses
	My own decisions
	My own judgment
Whom should I serve:	My children
	Their future
	Their health
	My family

Then answer the summary questions:

My Core values:
- Honesty, Work, Industry, Peace, Solitude, Independence vs. Arrogance Illegitimacy, Abuse, False Prophets, Vanity, & Waste;

What I Must Do:
- Not let my fear of control, regulation, power or authority interfere with my goal of freedom and education of children

What I must Learn:
- I must resolve my own doubts through inquiry and analysis to support and defend my beliefs

My aspirations:
- To be free of debt, to be free of pain, to be free of the practical details of civil society that seem utterly pointless to leading a meaningful life. In having this freedom, to have the time to explore the questions that interest me about life, to spend time with the people I care about, to spend time with dogs, and to do things that I find meaningful, rather than do things that are meaningless.

My sense of purpose:

I value hard work and I abhor waste. I believe in a divine being, but I am skeptical of false prophets. My goal is the happiness and health of my children, and freedom for myself, and to the best of my knowledge, I must work industriously for their future. I fear my own ignorance and doubt my ability to reason, but must overcome these deficits in order to be present with my children and not be consumed with worry about the things I cannot control, and will never understand. I must continually seek the wisdom of others, and with all humility, pray for guidance.

This is just the beginning. Take your time with this. Talk to someone you trust. Think about what it is you value, what is important. These questions really do matter because your answers will guide the Inventory. How does your purpose align with your life? This is where transformation becomes not just some vague idea, but a real possibility.

HOW TO DO THE INVENTORY

The Inventory is exactly as it sounds. It is an inventory of the people, objects, and activities that you do in your life. The question is, how do they relate to your purpose. Are they aligned with your values?

The worksheets included here give you a few ideas of where to start. You can catalogue things you own, people you spend time with, and things you do. Think about not the major "people" in your life, as in immediate family (it is a foregone conclusion that your children are likely very important to you) — but rather, people you spend a great deal of time with that you might not be thinking about consciously. This could be thought of in a number of ways — who do you communicate with online? Who do you write a lot of emails to? Who do spend a lot of time on the phone with? Are there people who routinely consume more time than others on a consistent basis either socially or professionally?

Give it some thought. List them out. Now do a simple exercise - how do they match up with your sense of purpose? There are a number of ways to check this. You have four different axes now, and four additional beneath, that provide insight as to what is important to you personally. How do these people intersect, unify, relate, support, or contribute with absolute necessity to either your Role, your Values, your Beliefs, or your Goals? If they don't, why on earth do you spend any time at all with them?

Now here is a fun exercise — the next time someone wants you to meet someone new, a business connection or a social connection, do this math in your head — assess how this person could relate to your purpose before you commit. Learn as much as you can; show genuine interest — be earnest, but if the math does not "add up" — then the answer should be clear to you. How many lunches, dinners, phone calls, emails and wasted social interactions must you pay for with your family's time in order to learn from a basic truth about your own self - you can determine who you need to meet on your own, don't let someone else dictate it for you.

This can be said of events, of books, of TV shows, of recipes, places to visit, things to eat, literally everything. The reality is that we are largely brought up with idea that sampling the world indiscriminately is to be celebrated; in point of fact, there is only so much time we have on this earth, and we must use our capacity for discernment to gauge its relevance to our lives, and its practicality within the framework of our existence.

The Inventory method I suggest here is based on rudimentary set theory. Either something belongs in the set in a fashion, or not at all. You can choose what you like, depending upon what makes most sense to you; the idea here is not to constrain you, but to free you from the tyranny of self-ignorance.

Example - The Inventory in Real Life

I use the Inventory in assessing my choices when I have difficult decisions, or when the choice is not immediately obvious to me. One of the most interesting observations about the Inventory is that it reveals the fundamental truth of what is absolutely necessary, and what is not, without making you judge yourself. Very often, we make choices based upon false assumptions about what we actually believe in, or what we think the right thing to do is. Here is an example:

Week of April 24, 2015:

Assumption: $500 in discretionary spending cash saved for "opportunities":

Charity Golf Game:
Time commitment: entire day. Cost: a hefty $250 (I don't even play golf!)
- Aligned with Values? Maybe.
- Aligned with Goals? Maybe.
- Aligned with Beliefs? Maybe.
- Aligned with Role? **No.**

School Project for daughter:
Time commitment, 8 hours, Cost: will miss big game on TV
- Aligned with Values? Yes.
- Aligned with Goals? Yes.
- Aligned with my Beliefs? Yes.
- Aligned with Role? Yes.

Drive to DC to hang out with college buddies for big game:
Time commitment: The weekend. Cost: who cares, right?
- Aligned with Values? Yes.
- Aligned with Goals? Yes.
- Aligned with Beliefs? Yes.
- Aligned with Role? **No.**

On its face, being "charitable" sounds like a great idea — but if it is cause you truly support, do you have to play golf (or pretend to play golf) in order to support it? What is the real motive for participating? How would taking an unscheduled trip away from home for the weekend actually fulfill my obligations to my family? Sure — we are supposed to have fun, but what is more important within this frame of choices? We often talk about priorities, but not understanding why something isn't aligned with your perception of purpose is just as important as knowing what is. If your goal is to be charitable, then be charitable; what is the *real* motive for spending the day on the course? And if you want to have fun — that is certainly allowed — but it should not come at the cost of your Role. What will be the price to your daughter in not helping her? Who *should* you be serving?

Obviously, doing this kind of exercise on paper is not what I expect anyone to do as a matter of practice, but doing it once to inspect the various people, things and activities in your life is immensely revealing. On the face of it, we split our time and our money as far as it can go, and then split it again, until it is strained to the point of insignificance; and then we wonder why things are so fraught. It is because of these relatively thoughtless decisions that go against our basic sense of purpose that we find ourselves trying to make increasingly difficult decisions between things that are truly important.

Also, my assertion is not that decisions are guided only by money. I use it as an illustrative device to frame the logic of the dilemma for the sake of convenience. The infinite number of possibilities between the decisions of your life and my own make it impossible to theorize a generality that would account for every nuance and variation. Yet, for every scenario, I assert that what will remain true as a constant in each equation is that if a given person, thing, or activity is not aligned with one of the four elements of your purpose, it should be added to your Inventory, and scrutinized with appropriate care.

The cost of critical self-examination is zero; the cost of acting out of ignorance of one's self is literally incalculable.

CHAPTER FIVE

Conclusion

WHAT I BELIEVE

I offer the following suggestions your consideration, as I think it is only fair that I offer some notion of what I believe given what I have tried to learn over the years. These are the ideas that guide how I spend my time, and make my decisions. What do you think of them?

- Do not confuse your goals with your purpose, and do not be swayed by every new idea that comes your way about what to do with your life. Your values, goals, beliefs, and role will no doubt evolve over time — that is a logical function of growth and change. However, continuous reflection upon the elements of your purpose will help shape the actions of your life, and how you perceive it.

- There are so many tensions in life, so many odds you will face, so many opposing views and so many questions of faith. Your compass is your integrity, but it will fail you if you are not honest with yourself first and foremost. Too often, we let others dictate our beliefs, our values, our goals, and our role – never settle for someone else's life. Decide these things for yourself.

- Understanding what your values are, your beliefs, and what you stand for, is as important as knowing what you don't believe in. Know yourself. Become familiar with who you are. Test your beliefs. Unlearn that which blocks you from learning more. Understand your motivations and the motivations of others around you so you can determine what is consistent with your values, your beliefs, your goals, and your role.

- Your purpose is ultimately defined by you, but it is shaped by your values, beliefs, goals, and role. Understanding the origin and truth of each of these things will guide the planning of your days – and your life. The honest pursuit of purpose, is purpose itself.

SOME FINAL THOUGHTS

The whole premise of this book can be reduced to a single point — self-examination, whether driven from a deeply religious point of view, or from a deeply philosophical one, is not incompatible with any faith, ideology, spirituality, or belief system, unless that that belief system requires you to be ignorant of yourself. What is shocking is that on either side of the intellectual debate, whether it is religious on one side, or so-called agnostic self-help on the other, do little to advance this age-old ritual of knowing oneself, and critically examining one's beliefs.   This abdication of our responsibility to knowing ourselves, what we do, and why we do it, has led to to the loss of the art of self-reflection, the loss of honest introspective inquiry, and the loss of self-knowledge. Adding more things to do, or more "Steps to Success" or whatever, is not my idea of an answer. Even worse, telling millions of adherents that it is selfish to rigorously examine oneself seems suspicious and unreasonable. If we do not question ourselves, we cannot be accountable, and if we cannot be accountable, we cannot improve. We cannot grow, we cannot learn, we cannot do a great many things that are part of being human. Ignorance is not a virtue.

I have always looked for simpler solutions to every

problem. I think dogs, for all their furry cuteness which is obviously a well played ruse, have been showing us a way out of the darkness, but we as humans have been too arrogant to learn from their example, and their wisdom. I think it is time that we start *perceiving dog.*

CHAPTER SIX
Workbook

THE WORKBOOK

The following pages contain the worksheet portion of the Inquiry and Inventory. For your convenience, space is provided for your notes as you work through each part of the exercise.

There are no "right" or "wrong" answers — but being honest with yourself is a key element to a successful and meaningful introspective process. The questions are posed as oppositional ideas deliberately, to help guide your thinking about what assumptions you might have about the four elements that compose your perception of purpose.

The premise of the Workbook is work through these steps in sequence:

1) The Inquiry - answer the oppositional questions that form the four elements of your purpose
2) The Inventory - apply what you have learned about the four elements of your purpose

The Inquiry is getting to the heart of what you know and what you believe; The Inventory is your own view of how your new conception of purpose matches up with the choices that you make every day, and throughout your life.

You will see two symbols on the Worksheets that follow, which are really just a suggestion, not a rule. The symbol that looks like an $\in$ represents what element or elements of purpose can be matched against the item you are interrogating; the Ω represents your decision about how it relates to your purpose. Is it relevant? Irrelevant? Does it intersect? Does it contribute to an aspect of your self that is critical? It is up to you to decide — but after doing the Inquiry, it is a fairly easy exercise.

There are no rules here; the framework I offer is just one way to look at how you can make decisions, and it is a practical one. If you have a method that works better for you, you should feel free to use it. The essential bit is this — **going forward, will you make decisions that are aligned with your perception of purpose, or will you ignore what you have learned about yourself?**

The truth can be painful sometimes — but if you want to change, you will need to understand the 'why' before you can do the 'how'.

It seems that dogs are able to make these decisions automatically and effortlessly. If you truly understand how honesty and fidelity are as natural to them as lying is to us, you will soon realize that our furry friends are bit wiser and a bit more conscious of their own reality, than we are of our own.

I sincerely hope this benefits you or someone you care about. I'm sure my dogs would have approved.

Good luck.

Sanjay Gupta

Elements of Purpose

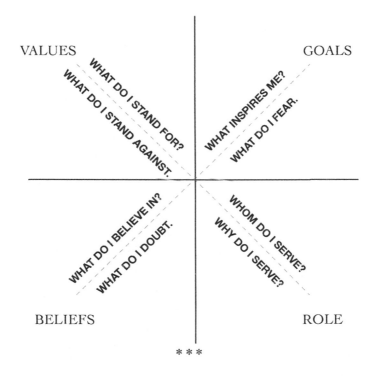

* * *

∴   Therefore

∅   Irrelevant

⊕   Optional

◊   Possible

Δ   Change

□   Necessary

∩   Intersects

∪   Unifies

Notes

INQUIRY

WHAT DO I STAND FOR?	WHAT DO I STAND AGAINST?
•	•
•	•
•	•

MY CORE VALUES.

-
-
-

Notes

INQUIRY

WHAT INSPIRES ME? | **WHAT I FEAR.**

-
-
-

-
-
-

MY ASPIRATIONS.

-
-
-

Notes

INQUIRY

WHAT DO I BELIVE IN?	**WHAT DO I DOUBT?**
•	•
•	•
•	•

WHAT I MUST LEARN.

- •
- •
- •

Notes

INQUIRY

WHOM DO I SERVE?	WHOM SHOULD I SERVE?
•	•
•	•
•	•

WHAT I MUST DO.

- •
- •
- •

Notes

INQUIRY

MY CORE VALUES:

MY GOALS:

WHAT I MUST LEARN:

WHAT I MUST DO.

MY SENSE OF PURPOSE.

NAME/DATE

Notes

PERCEIVING MY REALITY

This simple calendar exercise is based upon reflecting what demands are placed on your scheduled with respect to what is aligned with the four elements of your purpose.

Simply note what activities you typically do in the range of times in the calendar.
Next, mark if the activity is connected to one or more of the four elements of your purpose, Values, Beliefs, Goals, or Role.

You can use the rubric of the Logic that is offered, which is incredibly simplistic — either something intersects or is irrelevant; it joins, or it is essential. If an activity is not essential to your purpose, add it to your list of things to consider for review.

MY REALITY	M	T	W	TH	F	S	S
EARLY AM							
MORNING							
LATE AM							
NOON							
AFTERNOON							
EVENING							
LATE EVE							
NIGHT							

Notes

COMPARING MY IDEAL

This calendar exercise is intended to help you reflect on your conception of purpose.

Note what activities you would ideally like to do during the week, at the times you would like to do them.
Next, mark HOW the activity is connected to one or more of the four elements of your purpose, Values, Beliefs, Goals, or Role.

Did your your Ideal Calendar match up with your elements of Purpose?

MY IDEAL	M	T	W	TH	F	S	S
EARLY AM							
MORNING							
LATE AM							
NOON							
AFTERNOON							
EVENING							
LATE EVE							
NIGHT							

Notes

People I Spend Time With

	∈	Ω

Notes

Things I Spend Time On

	$\in$	Ω

Notes

Sanjay Gupta

Things I Own

	$\in$	Ω

104

Notes

Things I Want

	$\in$	Ω

Notes

Things I Lie About

	$\in$	Ω

Notes

Things I Want to Change

	$\in$	Ω

Notes

Suggested Books

	$\in$	Ω

Notes

Suggested Things To Do/See/Get

	$\in$	Ω

Notes

Suggested Meetings With People or Organizations

	$\in$	Ω

Notes

Other Considerations Worth Evaluating

	$\in$	Ω

Notes

ABOUT THE AUTHOR

Sanjay Gupta studied Philosophy at Georgetown University in Washington, D.C and did his graduate work at the University of Oxford, in the United Kingdom. He also studied Global Leadership and Public Policy at the Harvard Kennedy School of Government. In 2010, Sanjay was recognized by the World Economic Forum in Geneva as a Young Global Leader for his professional accomplishments and commitment to society, among fewer than 200 honored worldwide. Sanjay's career includes senior executive roles at Intel Corporation, as well as senior advisory roles to members of the Forbes 50 Wealthiest Americans.

A passionate advocate for the advancement of innovative childhood learning, Sanjay serves as a Trustee of the Sea Research Foundation in Mystic, Connecticut and Board Member of the World Affairs Council, which are both committed to educational excellence. He resides in Connecticut with his family and several pets.

Notes

Sanjay Gupta

Made in the USA
Monee, IL
30 March 2021